# Trash to

## 3rd Edition

# 90 Crafts That Will Reuse Old Junk to Make New & Usable Treasures!

### by Kitty Moore

Kitty Moore
ArtsCraftsAndMore.com

# Table of Contents

# Introduction

It is so satisfying to take a discarded item and make it beautiful and useful again. The projects in this book will teach you how to repurpose old dressers, drawers, pallets, tires, teapots, skateboards, and more! There are projects for your home and garden! Join the movement! Discover the inner treasure hidden in your trash.

# 1. Dresser into Towel or Fabric Storage

## Materials

- Old wooden dresser
- Electric sander and sandpaper
- Spray paint
- Primary color for the outside of the dresser
- Contrasting color for the inside of the dresser
- 5/8-inch MDF (Medium Density Fiber Board) for bottom of shelves
- Bead board (cut to fit the back of the dresser)

## Directions

1. Remove the drawers from the dresser. You can save them for another project. Sand the dresser with an electric sander until the surface is smooth and ready to paint. Remove drawer guides from the inside of the drawer spaces. Remove backing from the dresser.

2. Cut MDF boards to fit the bottom of the drawer spaces, and paint them in your selected contrasting color. These will be your shelves.

3. Secure shelves to the sides of the dresser. Paint bead board with your primary color, and nail it in place on the back of the dresser.

# 2. Dresser into A Bathroom Vanity

## Materials

- Solidly built old wooden dresser
- Paint or stain
- Leg levelers
- Cardboard or scrap board
- Razor knife
- Jigsaw
- 5/8-inch MDF (Medium Density Fiber Board) for bottom shelf
- 5/8-inch OSB Board (Oriented Strand Board) for vanity front
- Sink
- Countertop
- Faucet
- Hinges

- Wood screws

## Directions

1. Measure the length and width of the space where the vanity will go. Find a dresser that matches the space as closely as possible.

2. Remove the dresser drawers, and keep them for other projects. Remove lower drawer dividers in the dresser.

3. Attach leg levelers to the feet of the vanity. Make sure the vanity is the height that you want. You can cut the dresser legs if necessary. Make sure the vanity is level front to back.

4. Paint the body of the vanity. Draw a template of your sink on a piece of cardboard the size of your dresser top. Cut a hole for the sink with a razor knife.

5. Place the template on the top center of the dresser. Use a jig saw to cut the hole in the top of the dresser. Make sure the sink fits into the opening.

6. Make a cardboard template for doors and a false drawer to cover the front of the dresser opening. Cut the 5/8" OSB Board for doors and a false drawer.

7. Paint the doors and false drawer. Attach your chosen hardware to the doors. Cut a piece of 5/8-inch MDF to fit the bottom of the vanity. Cut the back of the vanity to allow for necessary plumbing.

8. Secure the vanity against the wall. Attach the faucet and water supply lines. Install the countertop and sink and secure them in place. Attach the false drawer and install vanity doors.

# 3. Dresser into A Bookcase

## Materials

- Old wooden dresser with tall drawer holes
- 5/8-inch MDF (Medium Density Fiber Board) board for shelves
- Corner molding
- L brackets for each shelf
- Paint (two contrasting colors) and paintbrush

## Directions

1. Remove the drawers from the dresser. You can save them for another project. Carefully remove the drawer guides from inside the dresser. Remove the backing of your dresser.

2. Cut MDF boards to fit the bottom of the drawer spaces, and paint them in your selected contrasting color. These will be your shelves.

3. Mark shelf placement. Attach L brackets at the front and back of the inside of the dresser for each shelf. Lay shelves on the brackets and level them.

4. Secure shelves. Cut corner molding to fit the front of each shelf. Attach the molding with finishing nails. Paint bead board with your primary paint color and attach it to the back of the dresser. Nail it into place.

# 4. Dresser into A Television Cabinet

## Materials

- Long wooden dresser
- Wood filler
- Primer paint
- Paint and paintbrush
- 5/8-inch MDF (Medium Density Fiber Board)
- Hardware
- Drill and screws

## Directions

1. The top of the dresser will be used for the television. The top three drawers under the top of the dresser will be used for the

videotape machine and other television accessories. The rest of the dresser will be used for storage.

2. Clean the inside and outside of the dresser thoroughly. Remove hardware from the drawers. Use electric sander to strip the top layer of paint from the dresser top.

3. Remove the three drawers under the top of the dresser and save for another project. Fill any holes with the wood filler and prime the dresser with the primer paint. Let the paint set.

4. Cut 5/8-inch MDF to fit the drawer spaces under the top of the dresser. Drill the required amount of holes in the back of the dresser for cables to run through.

5. Paint the wood for the shelves and inside box of the shelves with your primary paint color. These will be used for television accessories storage. Paint the dresser and remaining drawers. Reattach hardware to the lower drawers

# 5. Dresser into A Child's Toy Bench

## Materials

- Old dresser
- Bead board paneling
- inch lumber for supporting box
- ¾ inch plywood for back and side supports
- inch sheet lumber for the top of the bench
- Molding for the top of the bench
- Primer and paint

## Directions

1. Remove all drawers from the dresser. You will use the bottom layer of drawers. The rest you can save for a later project. Use a jigsaw to cut the dresser in half lengthwise. Remove drawer supports and separators from the middle section of the dresser.

2. Reinforce the inside back of the box of the dresser with 1-inch thick lumber. Support the sides of the box with wooden braces. Check to make sure the bottom drawers still move properly inside their frame.

3. Using ¾ inch plywood, build back and side supports about 12" from the box. Secure these supports to the inside of the frame.

4. Measure the top of the bench. Cut 1-inch lumber for this top section. Nail the top to the frame of the box. Nail the bead board inside the side and back supports for the bench.

5. Use finishing nails to attach molding to the top of the bead board and back and side supports. Remove hardware from the lower drawers. Prime and paint the bench and lower drawers. Reattach hardware to the lower drawers. Sew a cushion to fit the top of the bench.

# I have included a bonus just for you…

**FOR A LIMITED TIME ONLY** – Get my best-selling book "DIY Crafts: The 100 Most Popular Crafts & Projects That Make Your Life Easier" absolutely FREE!

Readers who have downloaded the bonus book as well have seen the greatest changes in their crafting abilities and have expanded their repertoire of crafts – so it is *highly recommended* to get this bonus book today!

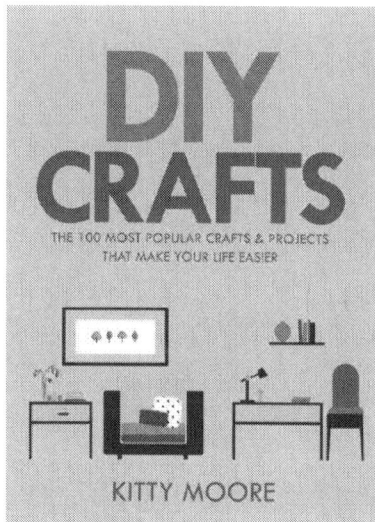

# Get your free copy at:

# ArtsCraftsAndMore.com/Bonus

# 6. Dresser into A Wine Bar

## Materials

- A three-drawer dresser with a wooden top
- Electric sander
- Pre-stain conditioner
- Wood stain
- Paint and paintbrush
- Wipe-on polyurethane
- 5/8-inch MDF (Medium Density Fiber Board) board for shelves
- Molding for the front of the shelves
- Hammer (optional)

## Directions

1. Remove the bottom two drawers and save for a future project.

### For the Bar Top

1. Sand the dresser top to bare wood. Distress the top with a hammer if you want to give it more character.

2. Apply a pre-stain conditioner to the top. Allow it to dry. Stain the top of the dresser. Apply a wipe on polyurethane.

**For the Wine Storage**

1. Cut 5/8-inch MDF Board for shelves where the bottom two drawers were. Paint the shelves and cabinet in a color that coordinates nicely with the stained wooden top

2. Cut molding strips to cover the front of the shelves and to provide a small ledge to keep wine bottles on the shelf.

3. Make or purchase two wine bottle holders that will fit inside each shelf. Stain the bottle holders to match the top of the cabinet.

# 7. Dresser into A Child's Dress Up Box

## Materials

- Old wooden dresser

- ½ inch plywood for the bottom of the box
- Batting material for the inside of the box
- Colorful fabric for the inside of the box
- Spring-rod curtain rod
- Wood glue
- Electric sander
- Staple gun
- Ribbon
- Plastic hangers
- Bright paint and paintbrush
- Small plastic bins
- MDF board
- Wall decals of your choice (optional)

## Directions

1. Take out the drawers from an old dresser. Save them for later projects. Remove the drawer supports, drawers, and backing of the dresser until all you have is the hollow box.

2. Sand the outside of the box until it is smooth. Measure the drawer holes, and mark the measurements onto your MDF board with ½ inch spare on each side. Attach the MDF board over the drawer holes using wood glue.

3. Paint the outside of the box a bright color, and attach wall decals for decoration. Staple batting material to the inside of the box. Staple fabric over the batting material. Cover the edges of the material with ribbon.

4. Place the curtain rod inside the top of the box. Hang costumes and dress up clothes here. Use small bins in the bottom of the cabinet for dress-up jewelry and other items. Attach decorative hooks to the outside of the cabinet for necklaces and hats.

# 8. Dresser into A Kitchen Island

## Materials

- An old wooden dresser with legs
- Paint to match your kitchen décor
- Blackboard paint
- Paintbrush
- Knobs
- 4 rolling wheels
- Paper towel holder
- Hooks for kitchen utensils
- Butcher block or laminate for the top of the island

## Directions

1. Select an old dresser that fits well into your kitchen and provides needed storage. Add wheels so that the kitchen island can be moved easily. Paint the front and sides of the dresser in a color that coordinates or adds a punch of color to your kitchen.

2. Paint the back of the dresser with black board paint. Add a handy paper towel dispenser at the top of one side and hooks for utensils.

3. Cover the top of the dresser with butcher block, laminate, or other recycled material that would make a good working center.

# 9. Dresser into A Pet Bed

## Materials

- Old wooden dresser
- Paint and paintbrush
- Cushion
- Electric sander
- 2-½ inch plywood boards for base and shelf
- Cushion to fit in the width of the inside cabinet
- Basket for toys
- Hooks

## Directions

1. Remove all the drawers from the dresser, except the top layer of drawers. Cut a ½ inch plywood board to fit inside the base of the cabinet. This will be the dog bed. Make or purchase a cushion to put here.

2. Cut a second piece of plywood. This will be used as a shelf. It fits inside the cabinet, just under the drawers.

3. Sand the dresser, shelf, and base. Paint the inside and outside of the cabinet. The top drawers can be used for pet supplies. The shelf can hold baskets for pet toys. Attach hooks on the sides of the cabinet for leashes.

# 10. Dresser into A Shoe Cabinet

## Materials

- Old wooden dresser
- Measuring tape
- Hand saw
- Electric sander
- 5/8-inch MDF (Medium Density Fiber Board) Board for shelves
- Paint and paintbrush

## Directions

1. Remove the drawers from a dresser. Build shelves from MDF to fit into the drawer space.

2. Sand the dresser and drawers. Paint the outside, inside cabinet, and shelves. Secure the shelves to the side of the cabinet. Fill your new shelves with shoes!

# 11. Drawer into A Bookcase

## Materials

- Large Drawer
- Electric Sander
- Paint and paintbrush

## Directions

1. Remove hardware from drawer. Sand the drawer inside and outside.

2. Paint the drawer inside and outside. Reattach hardware. Set the drawer on its side or mount on a wall. Fill your new bookshelf with great books!

# 12. Drawer into A Raised Storage Box

## Materials

- Four unfinished wooden legs
- Large drawer
- Bolts for legs
- Wood filler
- Paint and paintbrush
- Drill and screws

## Directions

1. Drill four holes in the base of the drawer at each corner. Attach the legs to the drawer with a bolt through the drawer.

2. Remove the hardware on the drawer and fill the hole with wood filler. When the wood filler has dried, sand the inside and outside of the drawer.

3. Paint the legs and the inside and outside of the drawer. Your drawer is ready to fill with toys or potted plants or craft supplies.

# 13. Drawer into An Ottoman

## Materials

- Large wooden drawer
- Four casters
- Plywood
- Electric sander
- 2 pieces of 2x4 inch lumber
- Paint and paintbrush
- Foam
- Fabric
- Staple gun

## Directions

1. Sand and paint the outside of the drawer and the wooden legs. Attach casters to the corners of the ottoman by drilling a hole on the inside of each corner.

2. Cut a plywood square that covers the top of the ottoman. Cover the plywood with foam the same size as the plywood square. Stretch a piece of fabric over the foam and staple to the bottom of the plywood.

3. Cut 2 lengths of 2x4 inch lumber to attach to the ottoman bottom and fit snugly inside the drawer. This will keep the cushion in place. Use the drawer space under the cushion for storage.

# 14. Drawer into A Planter Box

## Materials

- Drawer
- Scrap wood
- Wooden legs

## Directions

1. Use scrap wood to build two rectangular frames that are the same size as the drawer. These frames will add support to your planter box. One frame will be positioned at the bottom of the unit, and one will be in the middle. The drawer will be on the top for the planter box.

2. To build the rectangular frames, attach the shorter pieces between the legs first. Use wood glue and screws to hold the wood frames in place.

3. Secure the drawer at the top of the unit by drilling screws from each corner of the drawer into each leg.

4. Cut slats to cover the rectangular frame at the base of the legs. This will make a wood shelf that you can also use to hold a potted plant.

5. Paint the drawer and legs and slats. Drill three holes in the bottom of the drawer for drainage. Fill the drawer with potting soil, and add plants!

# 15. Drawer into A Nesting Box

## Materials

- Old wooden drawer
- Tea Pot
- Paint and paintbrush
- Twine
- Strong glue

## Directions

1. Paint the inside and outside of a wooden drawer. Glue a teapot base in the middle center of the drawer

2. For extra security, tie twine from the teapot to holes drilled at the top of the drawer. This will be the nesting box. The drawer will provide shelter for the nesting box.

3. Glue the top of the teapot to the bottom of the drawer. This will be a perch. Secure the drawer to a tree and wait for the birds to arrive.

# 16. Drawer into Under Bed Storage

## Materials

- Old wooden drawer
- Electric Sander
- Paint and paintbrush
- 4 Casters

## Directions

1. Sand and paint the inside and outside of a drawer. Attach a caster to the bottom of each of the four corners of the drawer.

2. Attach handle hardware so the drawer is easy to get out from under the bed.

# 17. Drawer into A Shadow Box

## Materials

- Small wooden drawer
- Two colors of paint (2 contrasting colors)
- Electric sander

## Directions

1. Carefully sand the inside and outside of the drawer until smooth.

2. Paint the outside of the drawer in color A. Paint the inside of the drawer in color B.

3. Use the box to display small collectables. Make several shadow boxes and group them together.

# 18. Drawer into Bathroom Storage

## Materials

- Narrow old drawer
- Electric sander
- Wooden dowel
- Scrap wood
- Stain or paint
- Paintbrush

## Directions

1. Sand and paint or stain the inside and outside of an old drawer. To make a toilet paper holder, drill on each side of the drawer, half way to the top. Thread a wood dowel through the holes.

2.  Make a shelf from scarp lumber cut to fit inside the drawer. Attach the shelf from the outside with screws. Hang the shelf on the bathroom wall.

# 19. Drawer into A Communication Center

## Materials

- An old drawer
- Electric sander
- Paint of your choice and blackboard paint
- Paintbrush
- Small cork bulletin board
- Cup hooks

## Directions

1.  Sand the inside and outside of an old drawer. Paint the outside of the drawer in a color of your choice. Paint the inside of the drawer with blackboard paint. This will be a message board.

2. Hot glue a small cork bulletin board inside the drawer. This will be a great place to hang a schedule, calendar, or coupons. Attach cup hooks to the bottom of the drawer. This will be a place to store keys.

# 20. Drawers into A Cat Playground

## Materials

- 5 old wooden drawers
- Long wooden table legs
- Electric sander
- Hand saw
- Paint of your choice

## Directions

1. Sand and paint drawers and table legs. You will make two attached drawer towers with staggering drawer steps so that the cats can climb from one drawer to another. You will have two drawers on one tower and three on the other.

2. Mark the height of each drawer. Cut the wooden legs to match the design.

31

3. Attach the wooden legs at the base and side of each drawer. Stack the drawer tables to achieve the design you planned.

# 21. Old Sweater into Warm Mittens

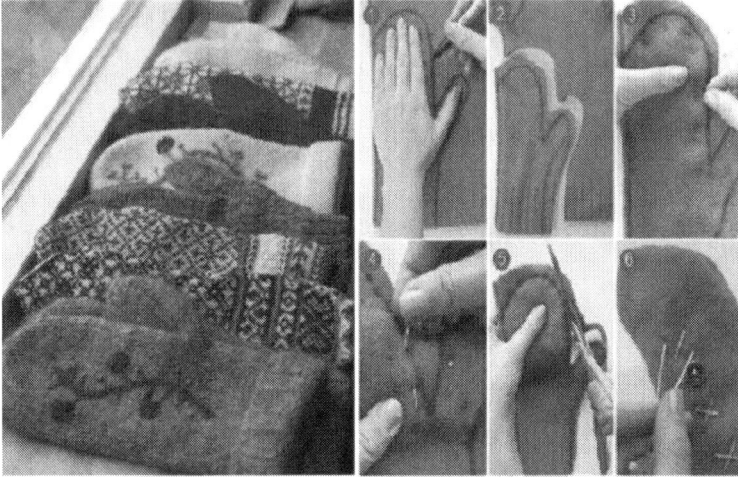

## Materials

- Old Sweater
- Pair of gloves to use as a model
- Sewing machine

## Directions

1. Place the sweater on a smooth, flat surface. Trace the outline of the mittens on the hem area of an old sweater.

2. Sew the shape of your mittens with a sewing machine before you cut the fabric. A 3.5-inch straight stitch will work well.

3. Cut out your mittens, turn them inside out, and try them on. If they are too big, you can sew them a little smaller.

# 22. Skateboards into A Headboard

## Materials

- 5-6 Skateboards (for a twin sized bed)
- 2-2" x 4" lumber pieces
- Stud finder
- Drill
- Long screws

## Directions

1. Layout the pattern that you would like the skateboards to be on the wall. Cut two 2 x 4-inch lengths of lumber the width of the bed. Lay the skateboards on top of the lumber pieces. Make sure they cover the lumber.

2. Use a stud finder to locate the studs in the wall where you want the headboard to be. Use long screws to anchor the lumber on the wall above the bed.

3. Place the lumber support beams 6" inches apart. Drill two holes in each skateboard into the lumber supports. Keep the drilled holes and the skateboards level.

# 23. Tire into An Ottoman

## Materials

- Large tire
- Rope
- Super glue
- Plywood
- Self-drilling wood screws
- 3 short wooden legs
- Metal top plates for wooden legs

## Directions

1. Wash a large tire to remove grease and grime. Starting at the outside of the tire, begin to superglue the rope to the tire, rolling the tire as you go.

2. After you glue a few rows on one side, start on the other outside edge. The last rows you glue will be in the middle. Cut two ply wood circles to fit into the middle space of the tire.

3. Attach the two plywood circles at the top and bottom of the tire with self-drilling wood screws. Attach 3 top plates to the bottom of the ottoman where the legs will go. Attach the legs

to the plate. Plan a rope design for the upper plywood circle. Trim the remaining edge with rope.

# 24. Iron Fence into A Side Table

## Materials

- Wrought iron fencing
- Metal L brackets
- Lengths of weathered boards

## Directions

1. This rustic table starts with a three-sided frame that you make from one long length of wrought iron and two narrower pieces at each end.

2. Connect the wrought iron pieces together with metal brackets on the inside of the frame.

3. Lay lengths of weathered board across the top of the frame for the surface of the table.

# 25. Drop Cloth into Patio Curtains

## Materials

- 2-pack of painter drop cloths
- 8 heavy washers
- Heavy wire
- Measuring tape
- Eye hooks
- Sewing machine or needle and thread
- Curtain rod clips

## Directions

1. Measure the length of the area where the curtains will hang. String curtain rod clips onto the heavy wire. Thread heavy wire between two eyehooks keeping curtain clips on the wire.

2. Cut and hem the drop cloth panels on a sewing machine or with a needle and thread. Drop washers into the hems as you go to give weight to the curtain panels.

3. Attach the curtain panels to the curtain clips. Curtains make great shade and can add privacy in the backyard.

# 26. Canning Jars into Patio Lanterns

## Materials

- Canning jars
- Duct tape
- White chalky paint
- One other paint color
- Tea light candles
- Paintbrush

## Directions

1. Cut out patterns from the duct tape and paste them all over the canning jar. Paint the jar with the white chalky paint. Use duct tape to make stripes around the jar. Paint with second color.

2. When the paint dries, carefully remove the duct tape stripe and the patterns you made with duct tape. Insert tea light and enjoy.

# 27. Pallet Wood into A Porch

## Materials

- Wooden pallets (number will depend on how big you want the porch to be)
- Electric sander
- Wood stain
- Deck screws

## Directions

1. Carefully dismantle the pallets and remove the nails. Plane the wood. Level the ground where the patio will be placed. Define the patio area with lumber frames, each 36" square and made with 2" x 4" lumber. Screw the frames together as the foundation of the porch.

2. Make a pattern for the 36" square to use as a guide for cutting the pallet wood. Cut 9 pallet wood pieces and screw to each frame. It will take 9 wood pallet panels per square.

3. Alternate the way the wood faces in each square. Continue making pallet squares until the porch frame is covered. Coat the pallet patio with stain.

# 28. Old Chairs into A Bench

## Materials

- Two identical wooden chairs
- 2 x 4-inch lumber
- ¾ inch plywood
- Foam
- Fabric

## Directions

1. Keep the back legs and back of the chair. Saw the front legs and chair seat away. Build a rectangular box the size that you would like the bench to be.

2. Screw the back legs and chair back to each end of the rectangular box at the level where the seat used to be. Build a

slatted shelf underneath the bench box and screw this to the chair.

3. Cut plywood to fit the top of the rectangular frame. Purchase foam to cover the top of the plywood. Cover the foam with fabric and staple to the underside of the plywood.

# 29. Wooden Chest into A Home Office

## Materials

- Wooden chest
- ¼ inch cork
- Cork glue
- Wood glue
- Molding
- File folders
- File folder case to fit inside the wooden chest.
- Craft box or wooden cutlery holder
- Paint or stain

## Directions

1. Paint or stain the outside and inside of the wooden chest. Attach ¼ inch cork inside the lid of the file chest. This will

be a bulletin board. Attach molding on the two long sides of the wooden chest with wood glue several inches below the rim.

2. Paint the craft or cutlery box to match the color of the wooden chest. Set the box filled with office supplies on the molding ledge.

# 30. Old Doors into An Arbor

## Materials

- Two old glass-framed doors without the glass
- 2" x 4" lumber
- Drill and screws
- Shovel

## Directions

1. Build a frame the width of the doors and the distance you want between the two doors.

2. Screw the frame to the tops of the doors. Dig an 8" trench on each side of the entry. Carefully place the doors in the trench and fill with dirt.

3. You can create a cap for the arbor from corrugated metal or scrap lumber or leave the arbor open to the sky.

# 31. Tire into a Flower Planter

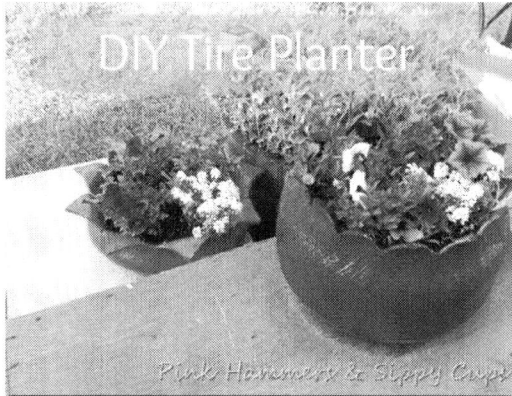

## Materials

- Old tire
- Sharp knife
- Mesh or chicken wire
- Spray paint

## Directions

1. Lie the tire on its side so it is flat. Using the knife cut out triangles, about 1 inch thick, from around the inside of the tire. The point of the triangles should face out. Continue to cut all the way around the inside of the tire. When you're finished, remove the inside of the tire.

2. Reach into the tire at the points and pull the top of the tire inside out. This will take some muscle power. Once the tire is

inside out, take the piece you removed and place it inside the bottom of the tire. Spray paint the outside of the tire and the inside of the points.

3. Line the inside of the tire with mesh to keep the dirt inside while still allowing for proper drainage. Fill your planter with dirt and plant flowers or vegetables.

# 32. Vintage Entertainment Center into A Child's Play Kitchen

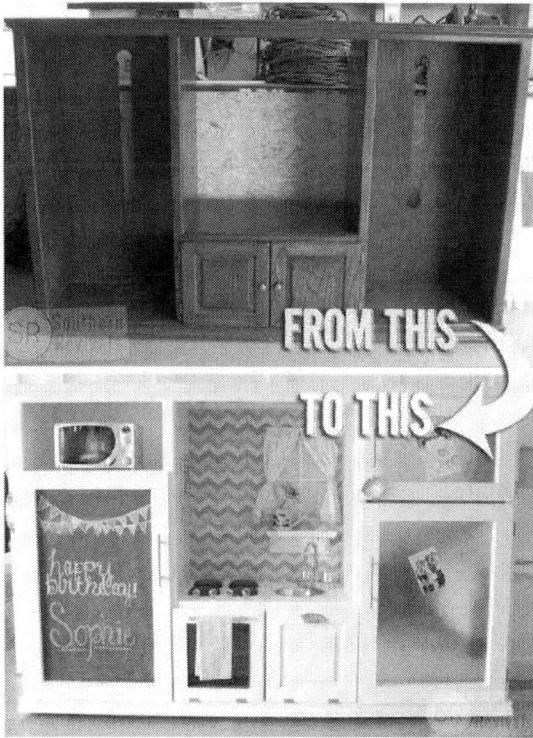

## Materials

- Large vintage entertainment center
- White paint
- Black paint

- Chalk paint
- Paint brushes
- Wrapping paper
- Fabric for curtains
- Small shelf
- Metal kitchen bowl

## Directions

1. Remove all of the doors from the entertainment center so all that is left is the frame. Paint the entire entertainment center and all of the detached doors white.

2. Paste the wrapping paper along the back wall of the section where the TV would usually sit. This will be the backsplash of the kitchen.

3. On the shelf where the TV would sit, you will have both the top of the stove and the sink. On the right half of the shelf, cut out a hole that is slightly smaller than the metal bowl.

4. Drop the metal bowl into the hole. This is the kitchen sink. On the left side of the shelf, paint four round burners with black paint. This is the stove. Reattach the doors under the stove and sink.

5. Using the black paint, paint the left cabinet to look like the front of an over. If you'd like, you can add fake stove knobs or hang a towel in front of the oven.

6. Reattach the other doors to the entertainment center. Paint one of the doors with the chalkboard paint. Once the paint dries, you will be able to write messages here in chalk.

7. Hang the shelf above the sink. Using the fabric, make curtains to hang above the shelf. Fill your kitchen with small fake foods or whatever your child would love!

# 33. An Old Lawn Chair into A Vintage Inspired Chair

## Materials

- Old lawn chair with a solid back and seat
- Sander
- White paint
- Deep blue or green paint

## Directions

1. Thoroughly clean the chair. Use the sander to remove any rust from the chair. Paint the arms and legs with a crisp white paint. It may take several coats.

2. Paint the body of the chair a deep blue or green. If you'd like, you can add a monogram to the top of the back of the chair with the white paint.

# 34. Upcycle an Old Bar Stool

## Materials

- Old wooden bar stool
- Polyester fiber filling
- Scissors
- Staple gun and staples
- Spray paint

## Directions

1. Spray paint the legs of the bar stool. Lay out the fabric on the ground upside down, and place the bar stool seat facing down on top of it. Place the desired amount of polyester fiber filling between the seat and the fabric.

2. Use the scissors to cut the fabric around the seat of the bar stool, leaving about three inches extra to attach the fabric to the stool.

3. Fold the fabric onto the bottom of the seat, and use the staple gun to staple it into place. Flip the stool back over, and enjoy your beautiful new bar stool!

# 35. Yogurt Container into A Succulent Pot

## Materials

- Yogurt container
- Rope
- Mod Podge
- Scissors
- Hot glue and glue gun
- Metal ribbon

## Directions

1. Thoroughly clean the yogurt container. Cut off the top third of the yogurt container and discard. Apply Mod Podge to the bottom inch of the yogurt container. Begin wrapping the rope around the container starting at the base (in the glue) and wrapping toward the top of the container. Make sure the spirals are very tight all the way to the top.

2. Once you are close to the top of the container, apply a generous layer of Mod Podge to the top inch of the container to press the rope into.

3. Allow the glue to thoroughly dry so the rope is fixed in place. Measure enough metal ribbon to wrap around the middle of the container. Secure the ribbon with the hot glue gun. Plant your favorite succulent in your new pot!

# 36. Tea Cup and Saucer into A Bird Feeder

## Materials

- Teacup and saucer
- Hot glue
- Chain
- Twine
- Charms or old keys
- Pliers

## Directions

1. Lay the cup on its side on top of the saucer so the handle is facing the ceiling. Hot glue the cup in place.

2. Run the twine through the loops of the chain to reinforce it. Attach the charms or old keys to the chain using the pliers.

3. Run the chain through the handle of the teacup, and attach it at the clasp. Hang the bird feeder on a strong tree branch. Fill the cup with birdseed so it spills out onto the saucer.

# 37. Thrift Store Finds into A Child's Play Room

## Materials

- Tall bookcase and small table (at least as wide as the bookcase)
- Paint (any color you'd like) and paintbrush
- Wood glue
- Wrapping paper (complementary to the paint color)

## Directions

1. Paint the bookcase and table completely white. Line the back of the inside of the bookcase with wrapping paper, and secure it in place with the wood glue.

2. With the table set firm on the ground, place the bookcase directly on top of it and pushed as far toward the back of the table as possible. Secure the two furniture pieces together with wood glue.

3. Fill the shelves with cups, plates, and other items your child will love to play with. They can use the table as a desk or countertop and the shelves like kitchen storage.

# 38. Old Doll Bed Frame into A New Doll Bed

## Materials

- Old doll bed frame
- Paint and paintbrush
- Fabric for pillows and blankets
- Scissors
- Electric sander
- Polyester fiber filling
- Needle and thread
- Wood glue
- High-density fiber foam

## Directions

1. Use the electric sander to completely sand down the bed. If necessary, glue in the wooden bed boards to the bed frame. If there are no bed boards or the bed is fully intact, skip this step.

2. Paint the bed your desired color. Cut out the high-density fiber foam to make the mattress. Wrap the mattress in your chosen fabric like a present. Use a little glue to hold the fabric together on the bottom side of the mattress.

3. To make the pillows, cut out enough fabric and sew them on three sides with the needle and thread. Fill the pillows on the fourth open side with the polyester fiberfill, and then sew the pillows shut. Cut out more fabric to make a top sheet or blanket. Make the bed, and enjoy the look on your child's face!

# 39. Old Brooch into A Cell Phone Case

## Materials

- Old brooch
- Clear cell phone case
- Pliers

- Rhinestones or beads (if desired)
- Super glue

## Directions

1. Remove the pin from the back of the brooch with the pliers and discard. Attach the brooch to the back of the cell phone case with the super glue.

2. If desired, arrange the rhinestones and beads around the brooch. You can arrange them in a pattern or randomly around the case.

# 40. Old Cable Spool into A Bookcase

Pandora's Craft Box

## Materials

- Old wooden cable spool
- Wood glue
- Fabric

- Batting
- Foam
- Wood for dividers
- Wood stain
- Staple gun

## Directions

1. Cut the wood pieces to fit as vertical dividers between the top and bottom of the spool. Each piece will need to be cut separately since the spool will be asymmetrical.

2. Secure the dividers in place with the wood glue. Stain the entire spool and new dividers with a dark wood stain. Cut the foam, batting, and fabric to fit the top of the spool. Place the foam on top of the spool.

3. Wrap the batting around the foam, and then wrap the fabric around the batting. Secure both the batting and fabric to the bottom of the wood with a staple gun. Fill your divided shelves with books, and enjoy your beautiful new shelf!

# 41. Pop Top Cans into Gift Wrap

diyinspired.com

## Materials

- Pop top cans
- Can opener
- Glue or tape
- Wrapping paper
- Ribbon
- Strong glue

## Directions

1. Use the can opener to remove the top from the pop-top cans. Save the tops. Empty and thoroughly clean the inside of the cans. Wrap the cans in the wrapping paper and secure with tape or glue. Wrap the cans in ribbon and secure it with glue. Fill the cans with whatever small gifts you want to wrap.

2. Secure the pop-tops back onto the cans with the strong glue. You might need to place something heavy on top of the cans to keep the lids secure while the glue dries. Your pop-top gift-wrap is now ready to be opened!

# 42. An Ugly Painting into A Headboard

## Materials

- Large ugly painting the size you want your headboard to be
- Old curtain panel
- Staple gun
- Scissors

## Directions

1. Lay the curtain flat on the floor with the nice side facing down. Lay the painting on top of the curtain with the front of the painting facing down. Cut the curtain around the edge of the painting leaving three inches in each direction.

2. Starting on one side of the painting, fold the curtain onto the backside of the painting and pull the fabric taught. Staple the curtain to the painting, leaving one staple every few inches.

3. Repeat this process for all four sides of the painting. Prop the painting back up, and enjoy your new headboard!

# 43. Old Glass Top Table into A Birdbath

## Materials

- Tall, circular table with a removable glass top
- Ceramic birds
- Large bowl (to fit the top of the table)
- Super glue
- Spray paint

## Directions

1. Remove the glass top from the table. You won't need it for this project, but save it to use for another project in the future. Thoroughly clean and dry the table. Spray paint the table your desired color. Place the bowl into the opening where the glass panel once rested.

2. Use the super glue to attach the ceramic birds to the edges of the bowl. Allow the glue to dry for 24-48 hours. Fill the bowl with water, and watch the birds enjoy their new bath.

# 44. A Plant Hanger into Stuffed Animal Storage

## Materials

- Large plant hanger
- Spray paint in a bright color
- Long strand of fake pearls (from your local craft store)
- Scissors
- Super glue

## Directions

1. Paint the plant hanger with the spray paint. Allow the paint to completely dry before moving onto step 2.

2. Wind the strand of pearl through the hanger to add embellishment. You can run the pearls up the sides of the hanger or through the basket portion.

3. Once you have finished wrapping the pearls, use the super glue to secure the ends of the strand into place. Hang your new storage unit from the ceiling of your child's room, and fill it with some of her stuffed animals. It's both whimsical and practical.

# 45. An Old Christmas Cookie Tin into A Decorative Storage Box

## Materials

- Large Christmas cookie tin
- Wrapping paper
- Mod Podge
- Paintbrush
- Scissors
- Ruler

## Directions

1. Cut out the paper to fit perfectly over the top and sides of the tin. You will need a separate piece of paper for each side of the tin. You can use the ruler to make sure your lines are perfectly straight.

2. Brush on a thin layer of Mod Podge to the top of the tin. Secure the top piece of wrapping paper to the tin. Paint a second layer of Mod Podge over the top of the paper. Allow it to dry completely.

3. Repeat steps on all sides of the tin. Once the entire box is covered and dry, you can use it for storage in your home or as a cute container for a gift.

# 46. Old Painting into A Ribbon Board

## Materials

- Old painting
- Ribbon
- Scissors
- Staple gun
- Fabric to cover the painting
- Pliers
- Paint (optional)

## Directions

1. Flip the painting over, and use the pliers to remove the staples from the frame. Remove the painting from the frame. Save the frame. You will need it later.

2. Pull the fabric taut over the front of the picture, and secure in the back with the staple gun. Paint the frame if you choose.

3. While your paint dries on the frame, lie the painting face up and begin cutting your ribbon into strips and lay them flat across the painting diagonally left to right. The number of ribbons will vary depending on the size of your painting. They should be a few inches apart.

4. Staple the top and bottom of the ribbons to the back of the painting.

5. Now, cut more ribbon strips to lay diagonally in the opposite direction. Weave them above and below the existing ribbon like you would for an apple pie.

6. Secure the new ribbons to the back of the painting with the staple gun. Once the paint has fully dried on the frame (at least overnight), reattach it to the painting. You will be left with a beautiful ribbon board!

# 47. Old Magazine Pages into A Fun Frame

## Materials

- Any frame
- Old magazines
- Scissors
- Mod Podge
- Tape
- Small paintbrush

## Directions

1. Cut the magazine pages the width of the frame. Roll up one magazine page into a small spiral. Secure the page with a small piece of tape. Make at least thirty of these rolls. You will likely need more, but thirty will get you started.

2. Once you have enough rolls made, begin applying them to the frame one by one. Attach them with Mod Podge using the small paintbrush. They should be side by side, running along the entire frame.

3. If needed, make more rolls and attach them until the whole frame is covered. Insert your favorite picture. This makes a great gift or a fun statement piece in your home.

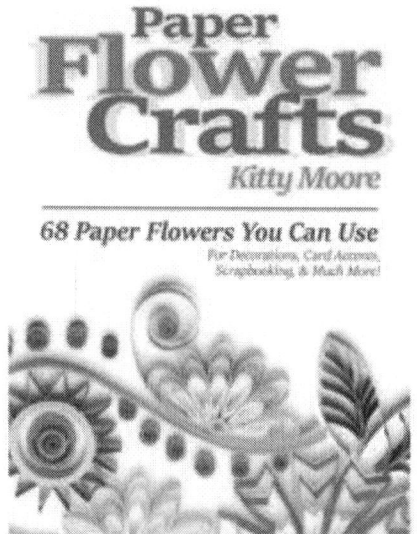

# Check out Kitty's books at:

# ArtsCraftsAndMore.com/go/books

# 48. Paint Sticks into A Lampshade

## Materials

- Lampshade
- Paint sticks
- Super glue
- Wood stain

## Directions

1. Attach one paint stick to the lampshade vertically. Secure it with the super glue.

2. Apply all of the rest of the paint sticks, side by side, until the lampshade is covered.

3. Once the glue has dried, apply a wood stain to the lampshade and allow it to dry. Place on your favorite lamp.

# 49. Pallets into A Sofa Bed

## Materials

- Screw driver
- Hand saw
- Double pallet
- 2 beams (240 cm long x 5cm thick x 10 cm wide)
- 4 furniture legs (30 cm high)
- 4 trolley wheels
- A slatted bed base (about 70 cm x 200 cm)
- 2 pieces of wood (about 2 cm thick x 10 cm wide x 80 cm long)
- Paint
- 2 Mattresses
- Screws
- Angle irons

## Directions

### Double Pallet (top part of the bed)

1. Place the beams under the double pallet. Secure the beams with the angle irons. Mount the legs to the double pallet.

2. Brush away any of the mess caused by drilling in the beams. Paint the entire double pallet. Allow it to dry completely. Then, flip it over so it is standing upright.

### Bed Base (lower part of the bed)

1. Flip the bed base over with the underside facing the ceiling. Attach the four wheels to the bottom. Secure them with the screws. Paint the bed base bed. Allow it to dry completely.

### Bedding

1. Place the mattresses on the double pallet and the bed base. Roll the bed base under the double pallet. Make the beds with whatever bedding you would like.

# 50. Pallets into an L-Shaped Sofa

## Materials

- 6 pallets (cut to the same width)
- Long nails
- Hammer
- 2 mattresses
- Decorative pillows

## Directions

1. Arrange two pallets on top of one another. Secure them with the hammer and nails. Repeat with two more pallets. Arrange the two double pallets into an L shape. Secure them with the hammer and nails. This is the base of the sofa.

2. Take the remaining two pallets and prop them up on their sides lengthwise. Prop them up behind the sofa at the place where the L curves. This is the back of the sofa. There should be a small length of sofa without a back. This is for aesthetic purposes.

3. Secure the back to the base with the hammer and nails. Place the mattresses on the base. Prop the pillows up in front of the back of the sofa. Lounge and enjoy!

# 51. Old Door into A Dining Room Table

## Materials

- Door
- Glass panel cut to the exact size of the door
- Drill and screws
- Paint or wood stain
- Chop saw
- Pocket hole jig
- Plastic floor protectors (for under the legs of the table)
- 4 wood panels (1" x 3" x 8')
- 4 reclaimed balusters

## Directions

1. Cut the reclaimed balusters the length that you want the legs. Standard dining table height is 29". So, subtract the width of the door (table top) from 29", and cut the balusters that length.

2. Lay the door flat on the floor. Place the balusters on the corners of the table for the legs. There should be one inch of table jutting out in either direction form the legs. Cut the wood panels to fit from leg to leg.

3. Drill three small pocket holes into each wood panel near the legs. Then, insert the screws sideways into these pocket holes so the screw runs from the wood panel to the leg.

4. Drill pocket holes along the lower part of the wood panels. Use screws in these pocket holes to attach the wood panels and legs to the table base,

5. Prop the table upright. Either paint or stain the tabletop (whichever you prefer). Once the paint or stain has dried, lay the glass panel on top of the door (tabletop).

# 52. Old Window into A Family Keepsake

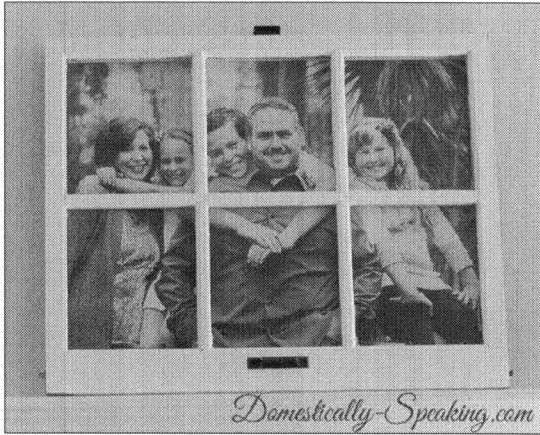

Domestically-Speaking.com

## Materials

- Old window
- Paint
- Family photo (same size as the frame)
- Cardboard
- Staple gun
- Mod Podge

## Directions

1. Cut the cardboard to the same size as the picture. Paint on a thin layer of the Mod Podge to the cardboard. Line up the photo, and carefully secure it. Be sure the press out any bubbles that form.

2. Paint the window your desired color. Apply the photo to the backside of the window (photo facing the glass), and secure it with a staple gun. Hang the window somewhere in your home. You'll love seeing it every day!

# 53. Glass Panel into Stained Glass

## Materials

- Glass panel
- Glass paint in multiple colors
- Lead adhesive strips
- Scissors
- Ruler
- Marker
- Backdrop paper (enough to cover the panel)

## Directions

1. Lay the backdrop paper over the glass panel. Cut it to the exact size of the panel. Using your marker and ruler, draw lines all over the paper to divide the space into a series of differently sized squares and rectangles. These will be your fake stained-glass panels.

2. Lay the glass over the paper so you can see the lines through the glass. Cut the lead pieces to fit the lines perfectly, and secure them to the glass. Recycle the backdrop paper.

3. Fill in the rectangles and squares with the glass paint. Be sure to fill the squares fully. Allow the paint to dry completely while the glass is still lying down. Prop your finished stained-glass panel up against an existing window or anywhere in your home.

# 54. Shutters into A Headboard

## Materials

- 4 old shutters
- Valspar weathered crackle glaze
- Saw
- Paint and paintbrush
- 2 wooden beams
- Hammer and nails

## Directions

1. Thoroughly clean the shutters. Coat the shutters in one layer of the crackle glaze. Allow the glaze to dry for one hour.

2. Apply a single coat of paint to the shutters. The crackle glaze will start to work immediately to make the paint look weathered. Allow the shutters to dry completely.

3. As the paint dries, line up all of the shutters in a row. Attach the two wooden beams to the bottom of the shutters to secure them together. Prop up your headboard behind your bed and secure it to the wall.

# 55. Shutters into A Kitchen Island

## Materials

- 2 reclaimed shutters
- Old drawer
- 4 rolling wheels
- Drill and screws
- Heavy cutting board (slightly longer than the drawer)
- 2 small hooks
- Paint and paintbrush (optional)
- 4 brackets

## Directions

1. The drawer will be the base of the island. The shutters will create the two sides. Attach the shutters to the short sides of the drawers so that the shutters jut up toward the ceiling. Use the drill and screws to secure them.

2. Lay the cutting board across the top of the two shutters. Use the brackets and screws to secure the cutting board to the shutters. Flip the island over and secure the 4 wheels to the bottom.

3. If you choose to do so, now is when you can paint the island your selected color. Stand facing the island so you are looking through it. Attach the hooks to the top of each shutter. These will be helpful for hanging towels, kitchen tools, or other small items.

# 56. Shutter into A Console Table

## Materials

- Reclaimed shutter
- 4 square wooden table legs
- 8- 2" narrow hinges
- 3- 1" x 4" x 8' wood boards
- 4 straight top plates
- Measuring tape
- Hand saw
- Electrical drill
- Electric screwdriver
- Rubber mallet
- Latex paint
- Paintbrush
- Pencil

## Directions

1. Brush two coats of paint onto each of the four legs. Allow the paint to thoroughly dry. Brush two coats of paint onto the front and sides of the shutter. The back of the shutter (bottom of the table) will not be seen, so you don't need to paint it.

2. Position a straight top plate into each corner of the bottom side of the shutter. Make sure they plates are all an equal distance from the edges of the table, as this is where your legs will attach to the table.

3. Screw the plates into the shutter. Screw the table legs into the top plates. Measure the distance between the two legs on the long side of the table, and write the number down. Repeat for the distance between the legs on the short side of the table.

4. Using the measurements you just wrote down, cut the wooden boards to fit between the legs. Place the first board between the short table legs. If it doesn't quite fit, use the rubber mallet to gently tap it into place. Attach two hinges to

each table leg (one on the short side of the table and one on the long side of the table). Once the hinges are screwed into place, prop the table upright.

# 57. Old Coffee Table into An Ottoman

## Materials

- Old coffee table with a drop-in glass top
- 2-1" x 4" wooden beams
- Wood panel the size of the inside of the table
- Hand Saw
- Measuring tape
- Drill and screws
- Paint and paintbrush
- Adhesive
- Foam
- Fabric
- 4 large fabric buttons
- Needle and thread

## Directions

1. Remove the glass panel from the table. Flip the table over and measure the distance inside from end to end. Cut the two

wooden beams the length of the table. Place one of the beams inside the table so that it crosses the middle of the table horizontally, and secure it with the drill.

2. Place the second wooden beam across the table vertically. Secure it with a screw on each side. This cross section of wood will provide the support for the ottoman.

3. Paint the entire table and allow it to dry completely. Place the wood panel inside the table where the glass panel originally sat. Cut the foam to fit directly on top of the wood panel (into the drop-down space of the table). Lay the fabric (nice side facing down) out on the ground. Lay the foam on top.

4. Cut the fabric around the foam, leaving enough space on all sides to wrap the fabric over the sides. It does not need to cover the entire foam cushion, just the top and sides.

5. Sew the buttons onto the top of the cushion. Make a three by three pattern. Use the strong adhesive to attach the foam cushion to the wood panel.

# 58. Old Deck Wood into A Laundry Crate

## Materials

- Old deck wood
- Wood glue
- Hand saw
- 2- 1" x 2" x 8' wood boards
- Electric sander
- Measuring tape
- Drill and screws
- 4 rolling wheels
- Wood sealant
- Pocket hole jig
- Paint and paintbrush (optional)

## Directions

1. Measure the area in your laundry room where you'd like the crate to fit. This crate will have space to fit two laundry baskets side by side with two above them. But you can modify the directions if you'd like it smaller.

2. Cut two large panels of wood for the base and the top of the cart. They should be the size of your pre-chosen space. Cut out twelve sections of deck wood and divide them into groups of four. Each group of four will be arrange in a square and secure to make the two outside walls and one inside wall of the crate.

3. Starting with your first four sections of wood, cut pocket holes into the sides with your pocket hole jig. Use the drill to screw the four pieces together so they make a square, like a big picture frame. Repeat step with the remaining groups of wood. You will end up with three squares.

4. Lay out one of your large panels of pre-cut wood (from step 2). Place one of your squares in the middle of the panel so it crosses the panel from front to back. Secure it onto the panel with wood glue, and then screw it into the base. Repeat step

with the remaining two squares, but on the far left and far right of the crate. These are your two outer walls. To make the basket gliders, cut the wood boards the depth of the laundry crate. You will need 8 totals.

5. Secure the gliders along the inside of each wall where the laundry baskets will hang. Leave about 1" of space between the top glide and the tabletop so the basket has space to be inserted and removed. Secure them with the wood glue. Once the body of the crate is complete, place the second large wood panel (from step 2) on top of the crate. Secure it to the top of the walls with both wood glue and screws.

6. Sand down the top of the laundry crate and apply 2-3 coats of sealer. You will do a lot of folding on this surface. The sealant will prevent your clothes from snagging on the wood. Turn the table upside down. Attach the wheels to the four corners with both wood glue and screws. If desired, paint your laundry crate. Allow it to fully dry before using.

# 59. Old Guitar into A Shelving Unit

# Materials

- Old guitar
- Paint (two contrasting colors) and paintbrush
- Drill and screws
- Handsaw
- Measuring tape
- Two pieces of plywood

# Directions

1. Use a handsaw to cut out the insides of the guitar. Leave the handle fully intact. Remove the strings and the entire front of the guitar. You will be left with the guitar shell and the handle.

2. Measure the depth of the guitar from the back wall to the now empty front. Cut your two pieces of plywood so they are the same depth.

3. Determine where you would like the shelves to cross the guitar. Measure the width of these sections, and cut your plywood to match.

4. Use the saw to make small divots along the inside of the guitar walls where the shelves will go. The divots need to be the same height of the shelves so they can slip into the sides of the guitar.

5. Paint the handle and the outside of the guitar one of your colors. Paint the shelves and inside of the guitar the contrasting color.

6. Once the paint is completely dry, slip the shelves into the divots in the guitar walls. Voila! You now have a brand new, extremely unique shelving unit for your home or office.

# 60. Old Red Wagon into A Hanging Wall Shelf

## Materials

- Old red wagon
- Saw
- Measuring tape
- Reclaimed wood beams for shelves
- Strong glue

## Directions

1. Saw the axel and wheels off of the wagon so all you are left with is the top "wagon" portion. Lay the wagon flat on the floor vertically. Measure the depth and width of the inside of the wagon. Cut the wood to match. How many pieces you cut will depend on how many shelves you want.

2. Apply glue to the sides of the shelves, and place them inside the wagon. Allow the glue to fully dry before hanging the wagon.

3. Once the glue has dried (preferably overnight), hang your new shelf on the wall in your home, or prop it up on its side. It's both charming and practical.

# 61. Old Doors into An Arbor

## Materials

- 2 reclaimed doors
- Paint and paintbrush
- 3-1" x 4" x 8' wooden beams
- Electric saw
- Measuring tape
- Drill and screws
- Pencil and paper
- Wood glue
- 4 L-shaped brackets
- 4 long nails

## Directions

1. Thoroughly clean the doors and remove any rust or nails. Prop the doors up side by side the distance that you would like them to be apart. Measure from the end of one door to

the end of the other door. Write this down. Measure the width of the doors. Write this down.

2. Paint the doors your chosen color. Be sure to paint both sides, as the doors will be fully visible from all sides. While the paint dries, begin working on the top beams.

3. Each wood beam will become one of the top beams of the arbor. Lay one of the beams horizontally on the ground. Measure out the length you wrote down for the total distance from door to door. Add another foot to this measurement so you can have 6" of overhang on each side. Cut the wood the new length.

4. Measure 6" in from each side of the newly cut beam, and use your handsaw to make a 1 1/2" high divot where the beam will slip over the top of the door. The width of the divot should be the width of the door. Do this on both sides of the beam. Repeat steps for the other two beams.

5. If you'd like the beams to have any sort of decorative design, feel free to cut them appropriately at this time. Otherwise, paint the three beams and allow them to dry fully.

6. Lay your doors on their sides so the top of the arbor is facing you. Lay the beams over the tops of the doors so that they are an equal distance apart. Secure the beams with wood glue, and they use the electric drill to screw them into place.

7. Place two L-shaped brackets at the base of either door (one in front and one in back, both facing the outside of the arbor with the second half of the L facing the ground). Screw the brackets into place.

8. Touch up the paint to cover the new screws and the brackets. Prop up your arbor where you would like it to go. Push the long nails through the brackets on the ground to act as stakes. These will help keep the arbor straight and sturdy.

# 62. Cans and Wood into A Silverware Holder

## Materials

- 6 recycled cans (all the same size)
- Paint and paintbrush
- 1" x 3" x 1' piece of wood
- Drill and screws
- 1" thick strap of leather (for handle)

## Directions

1. Remove the wrappers from the cans. This can be accomplished by soaking the cans in hot water for several hours. Once the paper is removed, thoroughly clean and dry the cans.

2. Paint the inside and outside of the cans. Make sure to use synthetic enamel paint since these cans will hold silverware that may be wet from the wash. Paint the wood with the same paint. Drill holes into the topside of each can.

3. Prop the fully dried wood on its side so that the widest part of the wood faces front and back. Line the cans up around the

wood so that three cans line one side of the wood and three line the other side. Drill the cans into the wood. Use a decorative pen to label each can with the type of silverware you'd like in that can. Lay the strap of leather across the top of the wood for the handle. Screw each side into place.

# 63. Liquor Bottles into Tiki Torches

## Materials

- 2 custom tiki torch wicks (from a craft store or Etsy)
- 2 clear glass liquor bottles
- Tiki fluid
- Matches

## Directions

1. Wash the bottles completely with water. Fill the bottles with about an inch of water each. You do not want the wicks to touch the water, so the exact amount of water will depend on the length of your wicks.

2. Fill the bottles with tiki fluid. Drench the wicks in tiki fluid and then place them in the bottles.

3. Light the wicks away from people, animals, and anything flammable. Once you are finished with your tiki torches, cover them with the wick lids.

# 64. Cardboard Box into A Play Oven

## Materials

- Cardboard box
- Scrap pieces of cardboard
- Box cutter
- Hot glue gun
- Spray paint for the color of the over
- Silver spray paint
- 4 condiment cup lids
- 4 small bottle caps
- 1 large bottle cap
- Full sheet of label paper

- Paper fasteners (brads)
- Blank or old CDs
- Black permanent marker
- Ruler
- Sheet protector
- Double-sided tape
- Plastic clothes hanger
- Battery powered light (optional)

## Directions

1. Turn the box on its side so that the lid opens in the front like the door of an oven. Cut a 13-inch square piece of cardboard, and glue it to the inside of the oven with hot glue.

2. Cut a 6 ½" x 9 ½" hole in the box lid to make the oven door window. Punch holes in the cardboard back for dials. Spray paint the entire oven and door with the desired color. Allow it to dry completely.

3. Spray paint the condiment lids silver and the bottle caps the same color as the oven. Attach silver dials to the range with paper fasteners. Hot glue the bottle caps to the lids, covering the fasteners. Hot glue the CD "burners" to the oven stove top.

4. Cut a 12 ½" x 9 ½" rectangle from the scrap cardboard, and spray-paint it silver. Allow it to dry fully. Draw lines along the length (about 1" apart) using the ruler and permanent marker. Fasten a sheet protector to inside the oven door with double-sided tape. This is where you can insert artwork to show through the oven window if you so desire.

5. Cut a piece from the clothes hanger and spray paint it silver. Allow it to dry, and attach it to the front of the oven with super glue to make the handle. Add a battery-powered light to the inside of the oven (if desired).

# 65. Old Window into A Distressed Mirror

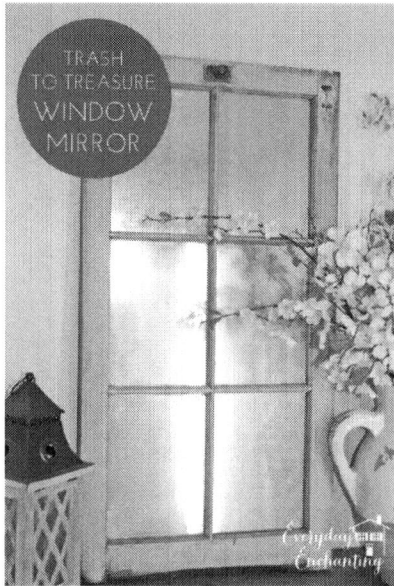

## Materials

- Old window
- Paint and paintbrush
- Vinegar and water
- Old towel
- Krylon looking glass spray
- Hand sander

## Directions

1. Sand down the window and clean the glass. Remove the glass for now. If the glass looks new, weather it with a mixture of vinegar and water. Just dab it onto the window with a towel and allow it to dry for a few minutes.

2. Paint the frame the desired color. Spray the glass with the two coats of Krylon looking glass spray, allowing it to dry

between coats. Put the glass back in the frame and prop up the mirror anywhere in your house that needs a lift.

# 66. Garden Hose into A Spring Wreath

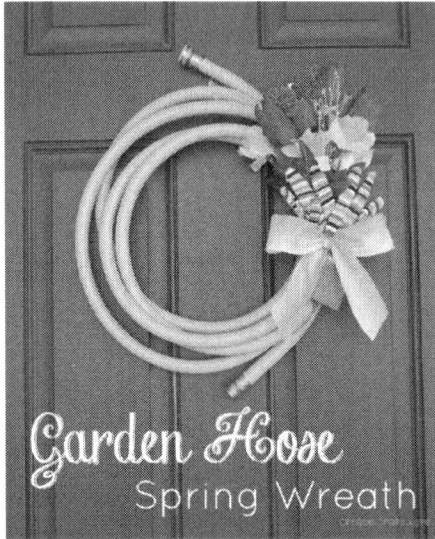

## Materials

- 15-foot garden hose
- Twist tie
- Silk flowers
- Butterfly clip
- Garden gloves
- Ribbon

## Directions

1. Coil the hose into a wreath-sized circle, and secure it with the twist tie. Stick the silk flowers under the twist tie until you like how it looks.

2. Place the garden gloves over the twist tie in a criss-cross position. Secure the gloves in place with the ribbon. Tie the

ribbon into a big bow. Attach the butterfly clip to one of the flowers.

# 67. Mason Jar into A Vase

## Materials

- Mason jar (any size)
- Mod Podge
- Scissors
- Fabric
- Pencil
- Paintbrush

## Directions

1. Lay the fabric face down on a countertop or table. Line up the base of the jar with the base of the fabric. Mark a line with your pencil where the top of the jar hits. Cut your fabric across where you made the mark.

2. Again, lay the jar on the fabric and roll it until the fabric fully covers the jar. Cut the fabric so there is a small overlap in the fabric.

3. Coat the outside of the jar with Mod Podge (using the paintbrush). Lay the fabric around the jar and smooth out any bubbles.

4. Apply another coat of Mod Podge along the outside of the fabric to seal it. Allow it to dry completely. Once the vase is dry, fill it with water and beautiful flowers!

**Note:** If you intend to use the vase for fake flowers only, you can insert the fabric in strips on the inside of the jar instead of the outside. It will look a little nicer and cleaner, but water will destroy it.

# 68. Tuna Cans into A Candle Display

# Materials

- 6 thoroughly cleaned tuna cans (labels removed)
- Scissors
- Wood hanger
- 6 tea candles
- Wrapping paper
- 6 wood clothespins
- Super glue
- Twine

## Directions

1. Cut the paper into strips to wrap around the tuna cans. Secure the paper with super glue.

2. Tie the twine around each can, and secure it with a bow and a dab of super glue.

3. Cut 6 pieces of twine in various lengths. Attach the twine to the bows on the cans. Super glue them into place.

4. Lay the wood hanger on the ground, and line up the cans under the hanger so that the open side of the cans face the ceiling.

5. Once you are happy with the arrangement, tie the pieces of twine onto the base of the hanger and secure them with the super glue.

6. Cover the tops of the twine with the wood clothespins.

7. Hang the hanger on your wall where you'd like your display. Place a tea candle inside each can along the rim. Light the candles. Enjoy the ambiance!

# 69. An Old Bottle into A Drinking Glass

## Materials

- Glass bottle you'd like to make into a drinking glass
- Nail polish remover
- Small bowl for nail polish remover
- Old towel
- Scrap yarn
- Lighter
- Sandpaper

## Directions

1. Prepare an ice bath in your sink. Put about an inch of nail polish remover into the small bowl, and set it aside. Wrap the yarn around the bottle at the place where you want the top of your glass. Wrap it at least 3-4 times. Make sure it is very tight. Tie a knot.

2. Remove the tied yarn, and soak it in the nail polish remover for one minute. Once the yarn is drenched, put it back around the bottle. Light the yarn on fire, and hold it horizontally form the base directly over the ice bath.

3. When the flame goes out (it will do so naturally), immediately lower the bottle into the ice bath. It should make

a clean break the first time. If not, just do it 2-3 times. It will eventually break. Sand the edges to make sure it's completely free of glass shards. Enjoy your favorite drink!

# 70. Globe into A Decorative Bowl

## Materials

- Globe
- Hot glue gun and glue
- Wooden plaque (for the base)
- Paint and paintbrush
- Knife

## Directions

1. Begin by removing your globe from the metal base and hardware. Usually you just need to gently bend the metal restraints and pull it free.

2. Divide the globe in half. There is already a seam down the middle where the globe was originally divided into two

91

pieces. Use your knife to gently separate the two pieces. Choose which piece you would like to use for your bowl. Either discard the other half or save it for another bowl.

3. Paint the wooden plaque your desired color. Allow it to fully dry. Attach the globe bowl to the plaque with a generous amount of super glue. Also add a dollop of glue to the inside of the bottom of the bowl where the hardware of the globe used to be.

4. Once the glue has fully dried, paint the inside of the bowl the same color as the base. Allow the paint to dry. Fill your new bowl with whatever you'd like (except food).

# 71. Old Porch Post into Candle Holders

## Materials

- Old porch post
- Hand saw
- Super glue

- Paint and paintbrush
- 4 candleholder plates
- 4 large candles

## Directions

1. Cut the post into four pieces of varying heights. Paint the pillars your desired color and allow them to dry fully.

2. Super glue the candleholder plates to the top of the pillars. Display them somewhere visible in your home.

# 72. Old End Table into A Dog Bed

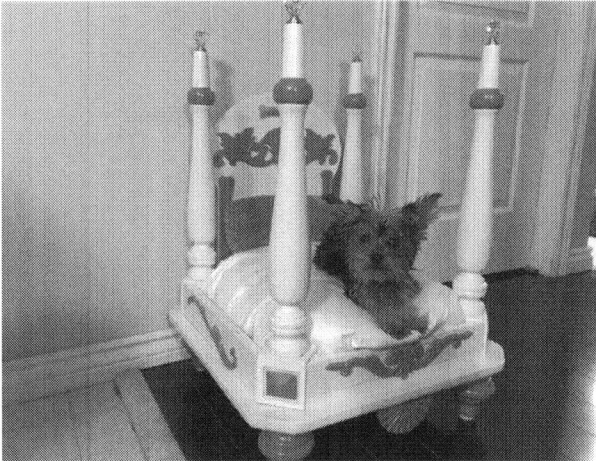

## Materials

- Old end table
- White paint and paintbrush
- 4 bun feet for the table
- Drill and screws
- Dog pillow the size of the table
- Plywood
- Wood glue

## Directions

1. Flip the table upside down so the legs are pointing up. Drill four holes into the corners of the table and then screw in the 4 bun feet so that the top of the table faces the floor with the four feet below it.

2. Cut the plywood to fit as a headboard between the two back legs. Paint the entire dog bed and headboard your chosen color. Allow the paint to dry completely.

3. Attach the headboard to the back of the bed with the wood glue. Place the dog pillow on the bed (underside of the table). Your dog will love it!

# 73. Tank Top into A Crop Top

## Materials

- Tank top
- Scissors
- Needle and thread

## Directions

1. Lay the tank top on the floor with the front facing you. Cut the tank in half horizontally. Gather the middle of the top half and sew the gathers together. Cut the bottom half to your desired length, and then cut the seam on the left side.

2. Sew the right side of the bottom half back to the right side of the top half. Leave 2-3" below the gathered portion. Sew the bottom to the top all the way around, and then sew up the left hand side again.

3. With the leftover fabric (from the bottom part that you cut off), make a little tie to wrap around the gathered part. You can also use a ribbon.

# 74. Cheap Wire Trashcan into a Rope Waste Paper Basket

## Materials

- Cheap wire trashcan
- Long length of rope
- Scissors
- Hot glue

## Directions

1. Secure the end of the rope to the base of the wire trashcan, using the hot glue.

2. Allow the glue to dry completely. Then wind the rope around the trashcan until it reaches the top. Secure the top end with glue and cut off the excess rope.

# 75. Old Chairs into A French Bench

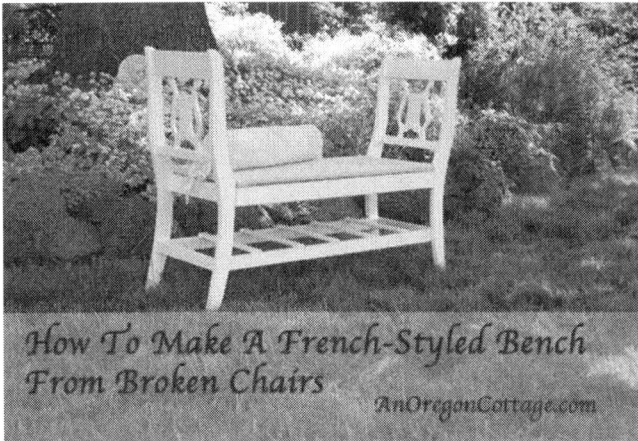

How To Make A French-Styled Bench From Broken Chairs
AnOregonCottage.com

## Materials

- 2 chairs that look good from the side
- ½" Plywood
- Hand saw
- 2" x 2" wooden beams
- Drill and screws
- Fabric
- Scissors
- Staple gun
- Futon cushion or pillows for the top

## Directions

1. Remove the screws from the chairs and take apart everything except the back and back leg of the chairs. This needs to be one fluid piece for each chair.

2. Make a rectangle for the bench using the 2" x 2" beams. Attach the bench between the chairs lengthwise. Attach the box to each chair by drilling through the back of the chair seat into the wood.

3. Create a bottom shelf using the rest of the 2" x 2" beams. Attach the shelf to the chair legs under the bench. Paint the entire bench and allow it to dry. Cut the plywood to fit over the bench frame. Wrap it in the fabric, and secure the fabric to the bottom of the wood with a staple gun. Place the plywood on top of the bench frame. Cover your bench in pillows or use a futon.

# 76. Old Wooden Chair into A Garden Plant Stand

## Materials

- Old wooden chair
- Spray paint
- Hand saw
- Large pot for flowers

## Directions

1. Cut the center out of the chair so the pot can rest on the frame. Spray paint the chair and the pot.

2. Place the pot on the frame and fill it with tall flowers and vines that can loop above the chair frame and over the sides.

# 77. Dining Room Chair into A Tree Swing

## Materials

- Old dining room chair
- Hand saw

- 2 long lengths of heavy rope
- Drill
- Paint and paintbrush

## Directions

1. Use the hand saw to remove the legs from the chair. Drill holes large enough for the rope into the two front corners of the chair seat. Run the rope through the two holes so the ends of the rope come out the top and the width of the rope is under the seat.

2. Drill another two holes into the top of the back of the chair. Run the second length of rope through these two holes so the width of the rope is behind the chair and the ends exit out the sides.

3. Looking at the left side of the chair, tie the front and back strands of rope together. Repeat step on the right side. You will now have two double strands of rope, one on each side of the chair. Tie the double strands to a large sturdy branch on a big tree.

# 78. Children's Car into Minnie Mouse Car

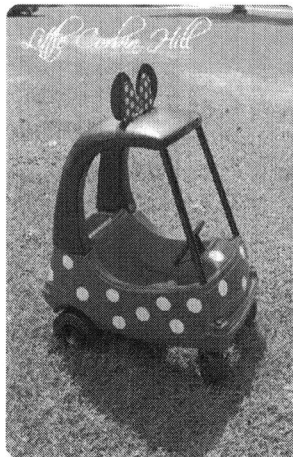

## Materials

- Children's car
- Red and black spray paint
- White craft paint
- Paintbrush
- Black craft foam (for Minnie's ears)
- 1/2" thick piece of plywood (for Minnie's bow)
- Glue gun and glue
- Hand saw
- Scissors

## Directions

1. Dismantle the car.

2. Paint the body of the car with the red spray paint and the beams, top, and steering wheel with the black spray paint. Allow it to fully dry.

3. Cut the plywood piece in the shape of Minnie's bow.

4. Paint the bow red. When the red paint has dried, paint white polka dots on the bow.

5. Cut the foam in the shape of Minnie's ears. Mount the bow in front of the ears, and secure them with the glue gun.

6. Paint white polka dots all over the body of the red car.

7. Reassemble the car. Secure the bow on top of the hood with a glue gun.

8. On the back of the car, carefully use the white paint and brush to write your child's name.

# 79. A Tire into A Sandbox

## Materials

- Used tractor tire
- Exterior paint
- Saw
- Strong glue
- Pool noodle (1.5 per 60" tire)
- Old sheet
- Sand
- Plywood cut into a circle to cover the sandbox

## Directions

1. Lay the old sheet down on the ground and lay the tire on top of it. Clean and paint the entire tire. Use the saw to cut along the inside edge of the tire to make the hole larger. Discard the excess tire that you remove.

2. Slice the noodle lengthwise halfway through so you can slide the opening of the noodle over the now jagged edges of the inner tire. Use as many needles as needed depending on the size of the tire, and secure them with glue.

3. Fill the tire with sand. When your children are finished playing at the end of the day, use the plywood circle to cover the sandbox.

# 80. Pipe Fittings into Candle Holders

## Materials

- Pipe fittings of different shapes and sizes (must have floor flanges)
- Spray paint
- Taper candles

## Directions

1. Wash all of the pipe fittings thoroughly. Assemble the pipe fittings however you'd like. Make sure the floor flanges are positioned as the base of the candle holders.

2. Once they are assembled to your liking, place the candle holders onto a drop cloth and spray paint them. Allow the paint to dry completely before inserting your candles and lighting them.

# 81. Wood Pallet into A Decorative Letter

## Materials

- Large wood pallet
- Hand saw
- Wood glue
- Plywood
- Hammer and nails
- Pencil

## Directions

1. Remove the wood from the pallet, and cut it down the middle to make 2.5" strips. Glue the pallet wood onto a sheet of plywood, and then nail the pieces into place.

2. Flip the plywood over so the plywood is on top and the pallet wood is on the bottom. Use the pencil to trace the letter you'd like.

3. Use the hand saw to cut through the plywood and pallet wood to create the letter. Use the remaining wood to frame the outside of the letter. Display it in a prominent part of your home.

# 82. DIY Baby Picture Frame

## Materials

- Square wooden frame
- Decorative paper (two different patterns)

- Pink paper
- 1/4″ wide brown ribbon
- 12″ x 1″ strip of burlap
- 1″wide button
- White thread and needle
- Super glue
- Alphabet tiles to spell out "baby"
- Mod Podge
- Paintbrush
- Scissors

## Directions

1. Lay the frame on top of the decorative paper (facing down). Trace an outline of the frame. Brush some Mod Podge onto the back of the paper and secure it to the front of the frame.

2. Cut out two squares of the second kind of paper. These will go in the middle of the left and right sides of the frame on top of the existing paper. Use the Mod Podge to secure the two squares.

3. Cut out several strips of ribbon.

4. Lay the ribbon flat at the intersection of the two different styles of paper. Secure it with a dab of super glue on the back of the frame.

5. Tie the strip of burlap into a nice bow. Sew the button onto the middle of the bow.

6. Super glue the bow to the top of the frame. Cut the pink paper into a rectangle to cover the middle of the bottom of the frame. Arrange the alphabet tiles on top of the pink paper. Secure them with the super glue.

# 83. Damaged Books into A Picture Frame

## Materials

- Old frame
- Old children's books
- Mod Podge
- Paintbrush
- Scissors

## Directions

1. Go through the books and rip out several pages of text. Cut out enough paper to completely cover the frame. Paint on a layer of Mod Podge to the frame and lay the text pages on top of it. Run the paintbrush over the pages to remove any air bubbles.

2. While the paper is drying, go through the books to find images that will fit onto the frame. Cut out the pictures as carefully as possible.

3. Brush Mod Podge onto the backs of the pictures and place them on top of the text. Fill the frame with your favorite picture of your child.

# 84. T-shirt into A Butterfly Twist Shirt

## Materials

- Old tank top (preferably a wide shirt)
- Scissors
- Needle and thread

## Directions

1. Lay the tank top on a table or other flat surface with the front facing down. Cut the seam of the left side from top to bottom.

2. Starting on the middle of the shirt, twist the left side several times so that the twist is in the middle of the shirt.

3. Sew up the left side again. You will be left with a shirt that has a big twist in the middle of the back.

# 85. Old High Heels into Glitter Heels

## Materials

- Plain pair of high heels
- Glitter of your choice
- Shoe glue
- Paintbrush
- Polyurethane

## Directions

1. Apply shoe glue with the paintbrush to the parts of the shoe where you'd like glitter. You can apply it to the whole shoe, just the heel, or in a pattern.

2. Pour the glitter on a little at a time and shake off the excess. Repeat this step several times until you get the amount of glitter you'd like.

3. Once complete, spray the shoes with a polyurethane spray to seal in the glitter.

# 86. Plain Shoes into Fabric Colored Shoes

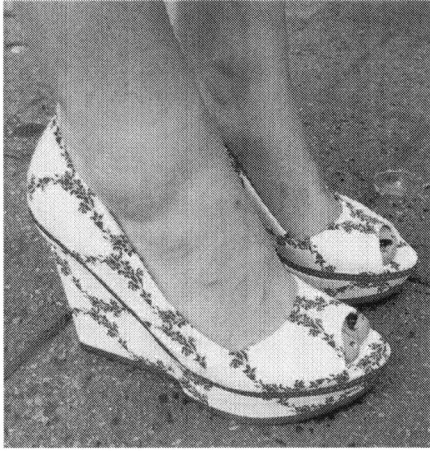

## Materials

- Plain pair of dress shoes (not strappy)
- Fabric of choice
- Thin cotton fabric to make the patterns
- PVA glue
- Pencil

## Directions

1. Prepare the shoe to be covered. If you have any straps that you don't want, rip them off of the shoe. Divide the shoe into sections. For instance, the toe, heel, and each side. You will need to cut a piece of fabric for each section.

2. Fold the thin cotton fabric around each section. Use the pencil to mark up where the lines of the shoe are on the fabric. Repeat this step for all of the sections.

3. Cut out the patterns from the white cotton pieces. dLay the pattern pieces on the thicker fabric, which you will use to cover the shoe. Cut along the pattern to get your shoe

coverings. Glue the fabric to your shoe using the PVA glue. Wear your new shoes with pride!

# 87. Chain and Scarf into A Halter Top

## Materials

- Chain
- Scarf
- Clasp
- Pliers
- Needle and thread

## Directions

1. Lay the scarf flat with the corners facing up, down, and sideways. Take the top corner and fold it over about half an inch (or less). Sew this together.

2. String the chain through the folded over area. Cut the chain to fit around your neck, and secure it with the clasp and pliers.

3. Sew up the bottom fourth of the scarf into a straight line with a nice hem. Your shirt is ready to wear. Clasp the chain around your neck, and tie the two ends in the back.

# 88. Old DVDs into A Mosaic Birdbath

## Materials

- Old birdbath
- Old DVDs (you can use CDs, but the color will be more subdued)
- Scissors
- Grout
- Strong glue
- Krylon crystal clear gloss

## Directions

1. Thoroughly clean and dry the birdbath.

2. Cut one DVD in half. You will see that it has two layers. Carefully separate the layers with your fingernail or something very thin. Discard the clear sides. You will only be using the shiny multi-colored side. **Note:** If you are using CDs, skip this step. CDs do not have two parts.

3. Repeat this step with all of the DVDs (enough to cover the inside of the birdbath). Spray the shiny sides of the DVD (the side that was inside when you opened up the DVD) with the Krylon crystal clear gloss. If you skip this step, the shine will be rubbed off and you will be left with dull discs.

4. Cut the dry DVDs into small pieces for the mosaic work. Begin gluing the mosaic pieces to the birdbath with the super shiny reflective side facing out. Once all of the mosaic pieces are in place, allow the birdbath to dry.

5. Next, apply a thin layer of grout to completely cover the gaps between the DVD pieces. Use a damp rag to wipe the excess away as you go. Let the grout dry, fill the bath with water, and enjoy your beautiful creation!

# 89. Colored Shampoo Bottles into Toiletry Holders

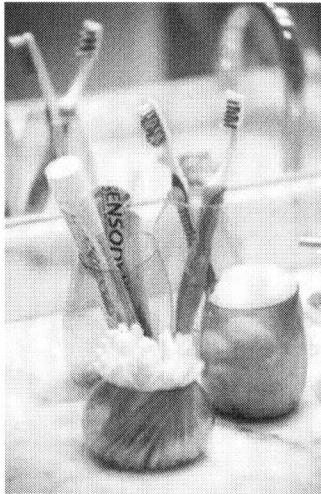

## Materials

- Brightly colored heavy plastic shampoo bottles
- Clothes iron

- Scissors

## Directions

1. Thoroughly clean the bottles. Cut the tops off of the bottles where you would like the openings of your containers to be.

2. Use a clothes iron on low heat on the openings of the containers. The heat will shrink the plastic, causing the openings to fold in slightly.

3. Arrange your new containers on your bathroom counter for a fun addition to your countertop storage.

# 90. Egg Cartons into Flower Lights

## Materials

- Cardboard egg carton
- Acrylic craft paint
- Sharp utility knife
- Foam paintbrush
- Hot glue gun
- String of Christmas lights

- Cutting mat

## Directions

1. Use the sharp knife to cut the egg carton. Cut lengthwise through the egg divots from end to end. Cut again from side to side crossing your knife over the egg divots. You will have five larger middle pieces and many smaller sidepieces. Discard the smaller pieces. For this project, you will only use the five large middle pieces.

2. Hold one of the larger pieces in your palm. You are looking at one of your flowers. Cut around the outside so that you have four "petals" rising from the base of the flower. Repeat step with the other 4 flowers.

3. Paint all of your flowers. Cut a small hole at the base of each flower. Push each flower onto one of the lights on the string so the flower tips point out. For a twenty light string, you will need to repeat this process with 4 egg cartons.

# 91. Toy Dinosaur into Bookends

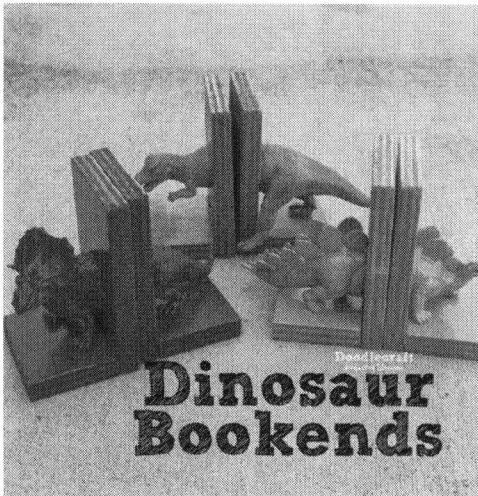

## Materials

- 2- 1" x 4" x 3" wood boards
- 2- 1" x 4" x 6" wood boards
- Plastic dinosaur
- Hot glue gun and glue
- Spray paint
- X-acto knife

## Directions

1. Use the hot glue gun to attach one 3" board to one 6" board to form an L shape. Repeat with the other two blocks. These are your bookends.

2. Use the x-acto knife to cut the dinosaur in half. Use the glue gun to secure the front half of the dinosaur to one bookend and the back half to the other. Spray paint the entire thing so it looks like one solid piece. Allow the paint to fully dry.

# 92. Cat Litter Bucket into Nautical Storage Tote

## Materials

- Cat litter bucket (cleaned and dried)
- 2 rolls of rope
- Hot glue gun and glue
- Silver spray paint
- Drill and screws

## Directions

1. Spray the inside of the bucket with spray paint. Wrap the bucket top to bottom with the rope. Secure the rope with hot glue at the top and bottom.

2. Drill two holes into the top of two parallel sides of the bucket. Run the rope through the holes to create a handle. Secure the rope with knots on the inside of the bucket.

# 93. Ugly Plain Planter into Vintage Inspired Wooden Planter

## Materials

- Large plastic planter
- Scrap pallet wood

- Brad nailer
- Wood stain (optional)

## Directions

1. Cut the pallets the proper length so they will line up around the planter vertically.

2. Secure the pallet wood with the brad nailer. If you desire, stain the wood. Enjoy your beautiful vintage inspired wood pot!

# 94. Lawn Chair into Macramé Chair

## Materials

- 600 ft of 6mm macramé craft cord
- 2- 19mm crochet hooks
- Metal lawn chair frame
- Scissors
- Lighter
- Macramé pattern

# Directions

1.  Remove the old backing from the chair and clean the frame.

**For the Vertical Weave**

1.  Starting on the seat bottom frame, make a double square knot, leaving about 6″ of slack at the end.

2.  Take your cord up below the center bar and over the top of the frame, then loop the cord over the top of the chair frame and pull it around to the outside. Push your crochet hook through the loop you just made.

3.  Bring the cord back down, underneath the center bar, and over the front of the seat frame. Wrap the loop over the frame and pull it under to the outside of the first couple of cords.

4.  Push the crochet hook through the loop, having it rest on the fat part of the hook. Pull the loose cord tight and continue.

5.  Now, bring the cord back up the chair just as you did before – underneath the center bar and up over the top of the frame. This time, pull the loop around the frame and back in between the cords. Grab the new loop with the crochet hook and pull it through the first loop, making your first chain stitch. Same as before, make sure this new loop rests on the fattest part of the hook. Pull the free cord tight and continue back down the chair frame.

6.  Repeat this same procedure across the frame until you've created enough cords for your pattern.

7.  When it looks like you need to do one more pass, take your cord and measure out how much cord it will take to complete the last pass. Then add about 6″-8″ to that length and cut the cord. To seal off the cord, cut it off, and seal it with a lighter.

## For the Horizontal Weave

1. The steps are exactly the same as with the vertical weave. The horizontal weave is where you will begin to see your pattern. You will start on the bottom seat and work towards the back and finish it off just as you did the vertical weave. Then you will start the back of the seat frame as a separate weave.

2. Just as you did before, begin by tying a double square knot to the frame, leaving about 6″ of slack. This is where your pattern starts, so weave your loop under and over across the chair until you get to the other side of the frame. Just as you did before, take the loop over the frame and to the outside of the cords. Push the crochet hook through and pull the cord to keep tight.

3. Work across the bottom of the chair until you've come to the end of the bottom frame. When you finish the pattern, end it like you did the horizontal cords by cutting the end and singing it with a lighter.

4. Start the back of the seat just as you did the bottom seat and the vertical weave. You will start this part from the base of the chair, rather than the top of the chair. Finishing the top of the chair is the same process as before. You now have a very unique and comfortable macramé chair!

# Conclusion

**Trash to Treasure** is a way of looking at the world— to find value in what someone else saw as broken or useless, to believe in possibilities.

Making new things from old, is not only good for the environment, it is good for us.

Our projects individualize our homes and reflect who we are.

# Last Chance to Get YOUR Bonus!

**FOR A LIMITED TIME ONLY** – Get my best-selling book "DIY Crafts: The 100 Most Popular Crafts & Projects That Make Your Life Easier" absolutely FREE!

Readers who have downloaded the bonus book as well have seen the greatest changes in their crafting abilities and have expanded their repertoire of crafts – so it is *highly recommended* to get this bonus book today!

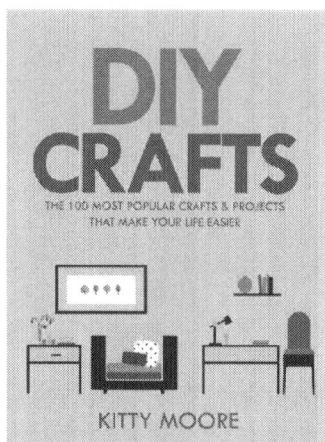

# Get your free copy at:

# ArtsCraftsAndMore.com/Bonus

# Final Words

Thank you for downloading this book!

I really hope that you have been inspired to create your own projects and that you will have a lot of fun crafting.

I do hope that you and your family have found lots of ways to fill lazy afternoons or rainy days in a more fun way.

**If you have enjoyed this book and would like to share your positive thoughts, could you please take 30 seconds of your time to go back and give me a review on my Amazon book page!**

**I really appreciate these reviews because I like to know what people have thought about the book.**

Again, thank you and have fun crafting!

# Disclaimer

**No Warranties:** The authors and publishers don't guarantee or warrant the quality, accuracy, completeness, timeliness, appropriateness or suitability of the information in this book, or of any product or services referenced by this site.

The information in this site is provided on an "as is" basis and the authors and publishers make no representations or warranties of any kind with respect to this information. This site may contain inaccuracies, typographical errors, or other errors.

**Liability Disclaimer**: The publishers, authors, and other parties involved in the creation, production, provision of information, or delivery of this site specifically disclaim any responsibility, and shall not be held liable for any damages, claims, injuries, losses, liabilities, costs, or obligations including any direct, indirect, special, incidental, or consequences damages (collectively known as "Damages") whatsoever and howsoever caused, arising out of, or in connection with the use or misuse of the site and the information contained within it, whether such Damages arise in contract, tort, negligence, equity, statute law, or by way of other legal theory.

Printed in Great Britain
by Amazon